Captain Blackboot and the Wallamagrumba

A Play for Children

Patricia Wood

SAMUELFRENCH-LONDON.CO.UK
SAMUELFRENCH.COM

ISBN 978-0-573-15223-8

www.samuelfrench-london.co.uk

www.samuelfrench.com

FOR AMATEUR PRODUCTION ENQUIRIES

UNITED KINGDOM AND WORLD
EXCLUDING NORTH AMERICA
plays@SamuelFrench-London.co.uk
020 7255 4302/01

Each title is subject to availability from Samuel French,

depending upon country of performance.

CHARACTERS

Captain Blackboot, an ex-pirate
The Bosun
The Mate
James
Sally } treasure-seekers
Victoria, a sand-castle builder
Black Jack, leader of a band of Wreckers
Fisheye
Ginger
Wreckers
Humphrey, a lion
Mrs Captain Blackboot
The Cook
Montague
Clara
Gregory
Liza
Samuel } Mrs Blackboot's children
Pansy
Percival
Egbert
Jemima
The Wallamagrumba, a denizen of the briny deep
Oliver, an octopus
Several Rows of Friendly People

The action takes place on a Desert Island in a
sunny Southern Sea

NOTES ON THE PLAY

Although this play is a sequel to *Captain Blackboot's Island*, it is entirely self-contained, and again very simple to stage. Any open space is satisfactory. It is also effective if the audience can be on three sides of the action.

Settings are minimal: a few "rocks" and perhaps one or two trees.

If a pianist is available, the excitement is increased by a few chords at the entrance of the Wreckers. Simple tunes may be invented for the Ballad of the Wreckers and the Children's Poem. These, however, are not essential; they come over very well if spoken.

The groups of characters, the Wreckers and the Blackboot children, can be expanded or contracted according to the number of actors available.

This play, like *Captain Blackboot's Island*, is of a good length for a complete entertainment for children—or the two plays together, with an interval between, can form a full-length performance.

Also by Patricia Wood published by Samuel French Ltd

Captain Blackboot's Island

CAPTAIN BLACKBOOT
AND THE WALLAMAGRUMBA

The sandy beach of a Deserted Island

One or two rocks are lying about and on one of them are three colourful feather dusters. Captain Blackboot sits sadly on another. The Mate wanders up and down carrying a Union Jack and a large ginger-beer bottle. The Bosun stands on the look-out rock, his telescope firmly fixed to his eye

Captain Blackboot Any sign of dear old Oliver, Mr Bosun?

Bosun (*changing his telescope to the other eye*) No sir. There ain't no sign, sir!

Captain Blackboot Dearie, dearie, me. Keep looking, Mr Bosun.

Bosun Ay, ay, sir.

Captain Blackboot How long is it since he's been missing, Mr Mate?

The Mate picks up a long stick with notches on it

Mate According to this stick, Cap'n, which I have notched up as faithful as can be, I makes it fourteen days.

Captain Blackboot Fourteen days without Oliver. It don't seem possible somehow!

Mate That's right, Cap'n. It don't.

Captain Blackboot Fourteen days without a sign of his little face. Nor none of his eight little arms. Did he have eight arms, Mr Bosun?

Bosun He did, Cap'n. Give or take a leg or two.

Mate It ain't natural! That's what it ain't!

Bosun (*shouting*) Cap'n Blackboot, sir! There's a sail on the starboard bow!

The Captain and the Mate move quickly to the Bosun

Captain Blackboot Where is it, Mr Bosun?

Bosun Three degrees to starboard, sir. It's a red one.

Captain Blackboot (*shading his eyes*) Can you see it, Mr Mate?

Mate No, Cap'n. I can't see it.

Captain Blackboot Neither can I, Mr Mate! Neither can I! (*He snatches the telescope from the Bosun*) Give me that! (*He looks through it*) No wonder you can't see anything, Mr Mate. No wonder! Seeing as how the Bosun has got a bit of red toffee paper stuck to the lens!

Bosun (*taking the telescope back and cleaning it off*) Sorry, Cap'n.

Captain Blackboot You wants to keep your equipment in better nick, Mr Bosun.

Bosun Yes sir.

Captain Blackboot Look how lovely Oliver kept his feather dusters. (*He picks them up*) Good as new, they are. Good as new. It brings tears to my eyes just to look at 'em. Which was his favourite colour, Mr Mate?

Mate I think 'e was fonder of the red one than anything, Cap'n.

Captain Blackboot So 'e was. So 'e was. And that's the very one as is missing! But 'e never neglected the others for his favourite, did he Mr Mate? He used them all strictly in turn.

Mate So he did, sir.

Captain Blackboot Put 'em back just as they was, Mr Mate. Just as the poor soul left them on the day 'e was whisked out of our sight.

Mate (*replacing the feather dusters*) Very good, Cap'n.

Bosun Do you think, Cap'n, that poor old Oliver got washed out to sea?

Captain Blackboot Washed out to *sea*? Use your common sense, Mr Bosun. An octopus washed out to sea? Suffering sharks, Mr Bosun, octopusses can swim like nobody's business!

Mate Then how did he go? That's wot I'd like to know. There weren't none of his dinky little footprints leading back there, into the jungle. And there weren't none of 'em leading down to the sea. So, how did he go?

Bosun Perhaps he grew a pair of wings and flew away.

Captain Blackboot You got less sense than wot you was born with. Whoever heard of a flying octopus?

Bosun Sorry, Cap'n.

Captain Blackboot Let's give Oliver a shout, Mr Mate. It might cheer the poor soul up a bit. And see if you can get a few friendly souls to help us.

Mate Very good, Cap'n. (*He walks down to the audience*) Ahoy there, Friendly Souls, will you help us give a shout for Oliver? Yes? That's very nice of you! After I've said go! One, two, three go!

Everyone (*shouting*) Oliver!

Captain Blackboot Once again, Mr Mate. The Bosun was a bit on the quiet side.

Bosun Sorry, Cap'n.

Mate Ready then? One, two, three, GO!!

Everyone Oliver!

Captain Blackboot He don't answer do 'e? (*He blows his nose on a large red handkerchief and walks sadly about the beach*) Oh dear, oh dear, oh dear. (*Suddenly he stops and gazes down at the sand*) Galloping grasshoppers! Mr Mate! Mr Bosun! Have a look at this!

The Mate and the Bosun hurry across

Mate What is it, Cap'n?

Captain Blackboot Footprints, Mr Mate! Footprints!

Mate God bless my soul!

Bosun Are they Oliver's footprints, Cap'n?

Captain Blackboot Use your loaf, Mr Bosun! Look at the size of 'em.

Bosun Big, ain't they?

Mate And look at the shape of 'em. Look at them toes, Cap'n! And look at them heels. They're like great knotted lumps of . . . I don't know what.

Captain Blackboot Bung up me brandy kegs! They're like nothing on earth!

Bosun Perhaps it's the footprints of an Abdominal Snowman.

Captain Blackboot Dust off me dandruff, Mr Bosun! What would an Abdominal Snowman be doing on a tropical island?

Bosun He could have got lost.

Mate Cap'n, I bin thinking. These footprints are leading straight to the jungle. Supposing this "whatever it is" has taken Oliver into the deepest depths of the jungle, and is keeping him there as a prisoner?

Captain Blackboot That's a nasty thought, Mr Mate.
Bosun Are you going in there and look for 'im, Cap'n?
Captain Blackboot And that's a nastier thought, Mr Bosun.
Mate Suppose we gives another shout, Cap'n? Just to let him know he's not forgotten?
Captain Blackboot That's a good idea, Mr Mate.
Mate (*to the audience*) Are you ready to give us another shout for Oliver? Good! Ready? One, two, three, *go* . . .
Everyone *Oliver*!!!
Captain Blackboot That was a bit on the loud side, Mr Mate. We don't want to upset the "whatever it is"—it might turn nasty.
Mate Very good, Cap'n. (*To the audience*) The Captain wants you to shout quietly this time. One, two, three, *go*!!!

This time the crew and the Friendly Souls shout very quietly indeed

Captain Blackboot That ought to do it! He ought to hear that! Back on watch, Mr Bosun! We can't leave a stone unturned!
Bosun Very good, sir.

The Bosun stands on the look-out rock with his telescope

Mate I can just imagine dear old Oliver, tied up to a tree, and slowly starving to death. It'll cheer 'im up to hear us shout like that!

The air is rent by a loud and terrible cry

Captain Blackboot (*trembling*) Jumping jelly babies! Is that your stomach grumbling. Mr Mate?
Mate (*indignantly*) No sir, it ain't!
Bosun Excuse me, Cap'n. I think it was the cry of the Wallamagrumba.
Captain Blackboot The cry of the Wallama-wot-a?
Bosun The Wallamagrumba, Cap'n.
Captain Blackboot And what's the Wallamagrumba when it's at home, Mr Bosun?
Bosun It's a denizen of the briny deep, Cap'n.
Mate Is it fierce?

Bosun According to my Uncle Charlie it's fiercer than a load of Killer Whales.

Captain Blackboot Wallop me wellingtons! I don't like the sound of that, Mr Bosun. I don't like the sound of it! Perhaps we'd better abandon ship, nip round the corner, and lock ourselves in the hut!

Mate We can't do that yet, Cap'n. It's four bells. Time for the ceremony of the flag.

Captain Blackboot Bunch up me begonias! There's just the three of us, Mr Mate. We can't have the ceremony of the flag with only three of us!

Mate Don't you worry, Cap'n. I'll find us a few more crew. Take a look through the telescope, Mr Bosun. Can you see anyone about?

Bosun (*looking through the telescope*) There's several rows of cheerful looking heads just above high water mark, Mr Mate.

Mate I'll have a word. (*He walks down to the edge of the stage*) Ahoy there, Cheerful Looking Souls! Can you hear me? Yes? Good. Captain Blackboot being rather short on crew at the moment, would be obliged if you'd join in the ceremony of the flag. Will you help us? You will? Very kind of you, maties, I'm sure. Do you know a song called "Rule Britannia"? Well, let's have a bit of a practice.

They do

Very nicely sung, maties! Now, when the Cap'n says one, two, three, go! You joins in the singing. Everything's ship shape, Cap'n. Just give us the word!

Captain Blackboot Ship mates all, 'tis time for the ceremony of the flag. Set up the colours, Mr Mate.

The Mate sticks the Union Jack in the ginger beer bottle

Whistle up the crew, Mr Bosun!

The Bosun does so

Now then—one—two—three—GO!

They stand to attention and all sing "Rule Britannia"

Captain Blackboot Well done, shipmates! Strike the colours, Mr Mate.

The Mate removes the flag from the bottle

Back on watch Mr Bosun! I'll just go and barricade meself into the hut.

The Bosun goes back to the look-out rock with his telescope

Bosun Too late, Cap'n. There's a wessel coming alongside the port bow!
Captain Blackboot Polish me plimsolls! Visitors at a time like this! Fend 'em off, Mr Mate. What we wants is to get tight and snug inside the hut before that there Walla-ma-wots its name comes climping and clumping up the beach!

James, a boy of ten comes running on, followed by Sally, who is nine and their sister Victoria who is seven and carries a bucket and spade

Captain Blackboot Well, bless my blazer buttons! If it's not them there treasure-seekers what was here last year!
Mate So it is, Cap'n.
James I hope you don't mind us turning up unexpectedly, Captain Blackboot! You see, there's an epidemic of measles at our school, and it's been closed down for a few weeks.
Sally So we thought we'd pay you a visit!
Captain Blackboot Welcome aboard, maties! Which one of you was it that found the treasure for us last year?
Sally That was our sister, Victoria.
Victoria Yes, that was me. You ought to remember *that*!
Captain Blackboot So I did ought to, Matey. That was a very clever thing you done—finding that treasure.
Victoria It was, wasn't it? Where is it now?
Captain Blackboot Ah well, you see, that's an awkward kind of a question, that is! Ain't it, Mr Mate?
Mate Very awkward, Cap'n.

Captain Blackboot We don't talk about it much, do we, Mr Bosun?

Bosun Not a lot, Cap'n.

Captain Blackboot It's like this, you see. Being busy at the time, building the hut that Mrs Blackboot had set her heart on, I got the Mate and the Bosun to hide it somewhere safe, somewhere that no human eye could look upon it.

James And did they?

Bosun We dug a gurt hole in the sand and dropped it all in.

Mate Piece by piece. Careful as if it was ostrich eggs.

Bosun Then we filled in the hole, and smoothed over the top.

Mate So as no-one would know there'd never been nothing there!

James That sounds sensible.

Captain Blackboot (*in a rage*) Sensible? *Sensible*?? So you might say, matie, if this double dose of dunder-headed dafties hadn t gone and forgot where they dug the hole!

Mate }
Bosun }   (*together*) Sorry, Cap'n.

Sally What a terrible shame. It was such beautiful treasure!

Captain Blackboot So it was!

Victoria Don't you worry, Captain Blackboot. I'll find it. It's a jolly good job I brought my bucket and spade with me. Oliver helped me with the digging last time, so he can help me again. Where is Oliver?

Bosun Gone.

James Gone?

Mate The poor dear soul 'ave gone.

Captain Blackboot Vanished off the face of the earth together with his favourite feather duster. A fortnight ago, it were, maties. And not a sign of him. (*He blows his nose and wipes his eyes*) You'll find us very sad here, maties. Very sad indeed.

Sally How awful!

Bosun He never left no footprints.

Captain Blackboot That's right, Mr Bosun—'e never did.

Mate One minute 'e was 'ere, and the next minute—gone!

Sally How absolutely terrible!

James What are you doing about finding him?

Bosun Well, matey, it's like this. I looks through the telescope, day and night

Mate And I notches up the number of days 'e's been missing, on
that there stick.

Victoria And what about Captain Blackboot?

Bosun Ah well. Sometimes the Captain sits and cries, and sometimes 'e just sits.

James That's not much use! We must find these kidnappers and
get Oliver back. Come over here all of you, and we'll work out
a plan.

*They are just settling themselves round one of the flat rocks when
the awful, terrible cry again rends the air*

James What on earth was that?

Captain Blackboot The Bosun says it's the cry of the Wallama-
wots-it.

Mate A dangerous denizen of the deep. Ain't that right Bosun?

Bosun That's right, Mr Mate. Beware of the Wallamagrumba,
my Uncle Charlie used to say! 'Tis a fearsome beast wot lurks
about in the briny deeps, disguised as a lump of seaweed.
Then, when it gets hungry, it bunches up its nasty knotted toes,
and comes climping and clumping up the beach, muttering
to itself.

Captain Blackboot Any idea what it mutters, Mr Bosun?

Bosun No, Cap'n. My Uncle Charlie wouldn't never tell us.
For fear, my Uncle Charlie said, of frightening us out of our
lives!

The fearsome cry again

Captain Blackboot (*panicking*) Abandon ship, all hands! Round
the corner and into the hut, maties! We'll bolt and bar the door
for a few weeks!

All Ay, ay, Cap'n.

Captain Blackboot And, Mr Mate . . .

Mate Sir?

Captain Blackboot Bring what's left of the feather dusters!

*They hurry after the Captain and presently we hear the sound
of the hut door being bolted and barred*

Sinister music

The Wreckers struggle up from the sea. They are a filthy and fearsome band, dressed in dirty striped reds and blues, with handkerchiefs or woollen hats on their heads. They carry kegs of rum and brandy and boxes of treasure. They put their booty down and render their ballad

The Ballad of the Wreckers

Wreckers   We're Wreckers all,
As you can see,
And we wreck the ships on a stormy sea!
We run 'em aground
By lantern light!
Then we takes our pick
In the middle of the night!

There's barrels of rum in the starboard hold!
There's a bale of silk and a box of gold!
And it's heave-ho! lads with the brandy keg!
But beware the sailor with the wooden leg!
Beware, beware, beware, beware
Beware the sailor with the wooden leg!

We're Wreckers all,
We know what's what!
As we plan our diabolical plot!
So keep away —
If you interfere,
We'll slit you throats
From ear to ear!

There's ruby rings in the skipper's bunk!
There's plates of gold in a leather trunk!
And it's heave ho! lads with the whisky keg!
But beware the sailor with the wooden leg!
Beware, beware, beware, beware,
Beware the sailor with the wooden leg!

*The Wreckers sit down wearily, leaning against the rocks. Black
Jack strides about among them, looking at their booty. He is
very cross*

Black Jack Never in all my born days, never 'ave I seen such a
weak, puny lot as wot you are. Never! Take two things each
out of the wreck, I says. You 'eard me say it! Two things each!
Wot's the good of me planning out the wrecking of a ship when
you only brings 'alf the stuff ashore?

Fisheye It were a bit cold in the water, Black Jack.

Black Jack Cold was it? You wants to wear your thermal under-
wear when you comes wrecking, Fisheye!

Fisheye Sorry, Black Jack.

Black Jack Two armfuls each next time, you lazy, loafing lot!

Ginger I can't manage two armfuls, Black Jack. Seeing as 'ow I
only got one arm.

Black Jack Then carry something in your teeth! Ain't you got no
brains, Ginger?

Ginger I ain't got no teeth, Black Jack.

The Wreckers laugh heartily at this

Black Jack Shut up! Who do you think you are, laughing before
I tells you to? Now, off to our cave where we stows the booty,
and lies low till nightfall. Then it's back we creeps with our
lanterns. Ready to catch the next ship wot crosses the bay.

*With many grumbles the Wreckers pick up their booty and
tiptoe quietly away*

*A rather moth-eaten Lion, wearing a golden crown studded with
jewels, comes from the direction of the jungle and down on to
the beach. He sits rather sadly on a rock*

Lion The King of the Jungle, that's what I am. The King of the
Jungle. King Humphrey the Heighth, that's me. (*He sighs*)
A large and powerful quadruped. That's what it says in the
dictionary. (*He sighs again*) King of the Jungle! And what's the
use of that? There's snakes in that Jungle, and I'm frightened
of snakes. There's spiders as big as your hat in that Jungle, and

I can't stand spiders. (*He stands*) Well, I won't be the King of the Jungle any more. So there! (*He takes off his crown and throws it down*) I won't be it! I'll go and be the King of the Ocean, that's what I'll be. They don't have snakes in the ocean! (*He picks up the crown and puts it on again. Then he walks sadly out to sea, muttering to himself as he goes*) I won't jolly well be it. That's what I won't. It's no good, I just won't! That's what! I'll jolly well go and be the King of the Ocean!

He is almost out of sight when he comes hurrying back to the beach

I never thought of that, did I? I mean, it never crossed my mind! I can't swim, and if I can't swim, I can't be the King of the Ocean. So I jolly well won't be the King of Anything! And that's that!

The Lion puts the crown on the beach then curls up behind a rock and goes to sleep

After a moment we hear the sound of People singing "The Grand Old Duke of York", and up on to the beach comes Mrs Captain Blackboot, her cook and all her nine children. She carries an enormous bottle of horrid looking medicine and a large spoon. The Cook carries a rolling pin. The faces of all the children are covered in bright red measles spots

Mrs Blackboot All children and Cook—HALT!

They do so

We'll give them a big dose of the measles mixture before we go any further, Ready with the rolling pin, Cook?
Cook Yes, Mum. I'm ready.

The children groan

Mrs Blackboot Line up then!

Very reluctantly the children line up. Cook goes behind the line of children tapping them on the head with the rolling pin. As each child opens its mouth and yells Mrs Blackboot shoves a spoonful of measles mixture down its throat

There you are. That'll get rid of the measles.
Montague It's ever so nasty, Ma.
Clara It's *horrible*, Ma.
Gregory Why can't we have ginger beer instead?
Liza Or orange juice?
Samuel Or lemon squash?
Pansy Or a sweetie to take away the nasty taste?
Percival I want a sweetie to take away the nasty taste, Ma.
Egbert So do I, Ma, so do I!
Jemima I want two sweeties, Ma, 'cos I'm the littlest.
Montague I want *three* sweeties, Ma, 'cos I'm the biggest!
Mrs Blackboot Be quiet all of you! Now, sit down and listen to me! I'm off to find your father, Ebenezer Blackboot. It's his duty to provide for his innocent children when they are struck down with infectious diseases. Now then, Cook, do you remember where that hut was that we made them build last year?
Cook Round 'ere somewhere, Mum. But I can't recollect for sure.
Montague Over there, Ma. Round the corner. Just where I dropped my lollipop.
Mrs Blackboot Now, Cook, you're in charge. And if one hair of their horrible little heads is harmed, I shall blame it on you. Understand?
Cook Yes, Mum.
Mrs Blackboot So mind yourselves.

She stumps off R

Cook Right you lot—I'm in charge, and I'm going to have forty winks! One peep out of you and you gets the sharp end of my rolling pin. Do you hear me?
Children Yes, Cook.

Cook and the children settle down in a heap and close their eyes. Montague soon gets bored with the idea of forty winks and leaves the heap to wander about the beach. The first thing he sees is the crown. Then he tiptoes back to Cook and taps her on the shoulder

Montague Cook!
Cook What do you want?
Montague There's a gold crown lying on the sand and it's got
  jewels all over it.
Cook No there ain't.
Montague Yes, there is!
Cook Go away before I bops you one!

Montague goes back to the crown and puts it on. Then he continues wandering about until he sees the Lion. He goes quickly back to Cook

Montague Cook!
Cook What is it now, you horrible little boy.
Montague There's a lion behind that rock.
Cook No, there ain't.
Montague Yes, there is!
Cook *There ain't!!*
Montague There *is!!*

The terrible cry of the Wallamagrumba shrieks through the air. The Lion leaps over his rock and, trembling with fright, clutches Cook tightly

Children (*screaming*) There's a lion! There's a lion!

They rush off R, *screaming. The Cook, still in the arms of the Lion picks up the refrain and yells "There's a lion, there's a lion, there's a lion!" Montague nips quickly back and bellows in the Cook's ear*

Montague I *told* you there was!

Montague follows the rest of the children off R

The Lion lets the Cook slip to the ground and runs around in panic-stricken circles shouting "There's a lion! Help, there's a lion!" Then he stands still and thinks for a moment

Lion That's me, that is! I'm a lion! (*Appealing to the Audience*)
Am I a lion? Am I? Well, if you say so, I *must* be a lion. Yes,
I remember now, I used to be Humphrey the Heighth, King
of the Jungle. Then I was going to be King of the Ocean,
until I remembered I couldn't swim. And now I'm just an
ordinary lion.

*During this Cook creeps up behind the Lion and gives him a
smart tap on the head with the rolling pin. The Lion sinks slowly
into unconsciousness and the Cook rushes off* R

*The Mate and the Bosun come from the direction of the hut
carrying the ginger beer bottle and the flag. They come towards
the audience*

Mate Take a look through the telescope, Mr Bosun. Can you see
if them Friendly Souls is still out there?

The Bosun gazes at the audience through his telescope

Bosun Still there, Mr Mate. Rows of 'em. All sitting in the sea
as neat as ninepence.
Mate I'll 'ave a word with 'em. Hello there, Cheerful Souls. It's
five bells, time for the ceremony of the flag. Are you ready and
willing to help us out again by singing "Rule Britannia"? You
are? Good. Friendly as anything, ain't they Mr Bosun?
Bosun So they are, Mr Mate. So they are.

James, Sally and Victoria come from the direction of the hut

James Is all well, Mr Mate?
Mate All's well, me hearty.
James No Wallamagrumbas Mr Bosun?
Bosun Nary a one, young sir.
James Then I'll call the Captain. (*He moves back a little, calling
towards the hut*) Captain Blackboot! All's quiet! We're waiting
for you to start the ceremony, sir!

Captain Blackboot appears. He is very nervous

Captain Blackboot You're sure it *is* five bells, Mr Bosun? We can go back and wait in the hut if it ain't. No sense in catching our deaths o' cold out here on the beach.

The Bosun licks his finger and holds it up

Bosun Five bells it is, Cap'n!

Captain Blackboot Polish me portholes, Mr Bosun! It don't seem right somehow to have the ceremony of the flag without dear old Oliver.

Mate Never mind that now, Cap'n. If we don't get on it'll be five and a quarter bells before you can say "knife". And you know how difficult that is!

Captain Blackboot Right you are then, maties. Stand to attention. Set up the colours, Mr Mate. Whistle up the crew, Mr Bosun. One, two, three, GO!

They all stand to attention and together with the audience sing "Rule Britannia"

Captain Blackboot Thank you, shipmates all. (*He wipes his eye and blows his nose*) Very nicely sung. Very nicely indeed. However it don't seem the same without Oliver singing the treble line. Always flat 'e was. Dear old Oliver. Always flat.

Victoria has been wandering about the beach and she notices Humphrey, who is still unconscious

Victoria Captain Blackboot, have you got an old moth-eaten hearth rug on your beach?

Captain Blackboot Batter me barnacles, miss. No, I ain't!

Victoria Then I rather think this is a dead lion.

Mate You will 'ave your little joke, miss.

Victoria It's not a joke. Come and see for yourselves.

Captain Blackboot I don't think I will, miss, if it's all the same to you.

James Don't worry, Captain. I'll look at it. She's probably exaggerating as usual.

*James, followed by Sally, crosses to where Victoria is standing.
They look down at Humphrey*

Victoria You see? I'm not exaggerating.
James It does look a bit like a lion.
Sally It looks very much like a lion.
Victoria It is a lion. A dead one.
Bosun Are you sure it's dead, miss?
Victoria Shall I poke it and see?
Everyone *No*!!!
Sally Poor thing. I wonder how it died?
Lion (*suddenly sitting up*) I got bopped on the head with a
   rolling pin!

Captain Blackboot and the crew move back

James It isn't dead at all!
Sally Oh, good!
Captain Blackboot It's alive, is it, Mr Mate?
Mate I reckon it is, Cap'n.
Captain Blackboot Mr Bosun?
Bosun (*looking at it through his telescope*) No doubt about it,
   Cap'n. I can see the whites of its eyes.
Captain Blackboot (*in a terrible panic*) Abandon ship all hands!!!
   Every man for himself!!! Except for the Mate and the Bosun
   who will at all times stay close to me! *Run for your lives*!!!

The three of them disappear towards the jungle

The Lion shivers

Sally It's shivering!
Victoria Perhaps it's afraid of us.
James There's no need to be. We're quite friendly. Have you got
   a name?
Lion Humphrey.
Sally What a lovely name!
Victoria I think it's a rotten name.
James Don't be rude, Victoria.
Sally Come along, Humphrey, we'll take you into the hut to
   get warm.

James Someone ought to stay out here on watch, in case the
   Captain and Crew come back.
Victoria I will. It's time I started looking for this treasure.
James Good. Knock three times when you want us to open
   the door.

*Sally and James take Humphrey away into the hut. Victoria
wanders about looking for a good place to dig*

*She has just made a start by the lion rock when Mrs Blackboot,
Cook and all the children tear out of the jungle, run across the
stage and exit. As they run they are all still screaming, "There's
a lion, there's a lion!". Jemima is now wearing the crown*

Victoria What a fuss people make about nothing.

*She gets on with her digging behind the rock where she cannot
be seen*

The Wreckers enter carrying lanterns

Black Jack Now then you frowsty looking lot, sit down quiet and
   listen to me!
All Yes, Black Jack.

They sit

Black Jack There's a ship running through the channel tonight,
   heavy with a cargo of brandy. She's bin sighted off Bloater
   Paste Rock, and should slide past Blue Nose Bar as darkness
   falls. Wot we want is to lure 'em on to the rocks in Skelington
   Bay, and let the tide carry the kegs o' brandy on to this beach.
   So when you 'ears the signal from me you lights your lanterns
   and waves 'em in the air. Then, as soon as she founders
   on the rocks, you nips back 'ere to pick up the booty. Is
   that clear?
All Yes, Black Jack.
Black Jack And if all goes well it'll be octopus stew for supper.
   Made out o' that nice plump little one we got tied up in the
   cave. 'E should be very tasty. Very tasty indeed! Off you goes

then, as quiet as a hatful of dead mice. Fisheye and Ginger stays 'ere with me.

A Wrecker Excuse me, Black Jack wot is the signal?

Black Jack Pin back your ears and I'll show you.

Black Jack puts his fingers in his mouth, but whatever noise he was going to make is drowned by the terrible cry of the Wallamagrumba

During the cry all the Wreckers disappear, except for Fisheye and Ginger, who, one each side of Black Jack, tremble behind a rock with only their heads showing above it

Fisheye That was a nasty noise, Black Jack.

Ginger Wot do you reckon it is?

Black Jack 'Tis the cry of the fearsome Wallamagrumba when searching for food. It comes rising up out o' the sea and climping and clumping up the beach. They say 'tis a terrible sight to catch the gleam of its ugly teeth.

Another cry worse than before

Black Jack 'Tis getting closer. Back to the cave!

The three of them make a bolt for it

The sky grows darker and a luminous light appears over the sea

The Wallamagrumba comes climping and clumping up on to the beach. It is indeed an ugly and a fearsome sight; its hair is a tangled mass of bladderwrack, long strands of seaweed hang from its neck to its knees, its large toes are knotted like the knotted roots of seaweed and its face is covered in large green barnacles. It stares hard at the audience

Wallamagrumba Heads. Rows and rows of human heads. What a pity they're not nice enough to eat. Any head is tastier than a human head. There's shrimps' heads and cods' heads, and whales' heads, all very good to eat. But the head of a bloater, that's a different matter. The head of a bloater served on a bed of stir-fried sea-worms, that's a treat, that is. (*He goes even closer to the audience*) Do you think I'm ugly? Do you? What? You do? Everybody does. It's not fair. I'm no uglier than you are. And I'm a better colour. You ought to see my two little daughters, Windy and Wosie. Purtier than a couple of sea anemones, they are. And my wife Winnie, she's beautiful, she is. (*He holds up Oliver's red feather duster*) This is a present for my wife Winnie. She'll like that, she will. I found it wandering about attached to an octopus. I grabbed both of them, but the octopus ran away into a cave. Still, I got this nice present for Winnie!

Victoria leaps out from behind the rock and grabs the end of the feather duster

Victoria (*pulling at it*) That feather duster belongs to Oliver!
Wallamagrumba Oh, no it don't! It belongs to my Winnie!
Victoria It belongs to Oliver!
Wallamagrumba It belongs to Winnie!
Victoria Oliver!
Wallamagrumba Winnie!
Victoria Oliver, Oliver, Oliver!!!
Wallamagrumba Winnie, Winnie, Winnie!!!

The cry of a Wallamagrumba rips through the air. They both stop pulling and listen

Wallamagrumba That'll be Winnie calling me in to dinner. But so far I haven't found anything to take back that's worth eating. (*He looks thoughtfully at Victoria, and walks round her a couple of times*) I don't know, though—we could always remove the head before cooking.
Victoria (*moving away a bit and holding up her spade*) You keep away from me or I'll bop you one with my spade!
Wallamagrumba (*quickly picking up the feather duster*) Yah! Yah! Yah! This is for my Winnie! (*He rushes down through the audience; yelling*) Winnie! Winnie! I got a present for you, Winnie!
Victoria (*yelling after him*) I'll get it back, so there!
Victoria Now I must tell the others that poor Oliver is a prisoner

in one of the caves, and he is about to be made into octopus stew!

She hurries off towards the hut

Mrs Blackboot, Cook and the children, still shouting "There's a lion, there's a lion!", rush across the stage from L *to* R, *Jemima still wearing the crown. They pass, without noticing Captain Blackboot and his crew, also shouting "There's a lion, there's a lion!", who are rushing across the stage from* R *to* L

There is silence for a moment and then the two parties rush on again, this time with Samuel wearing the crown and they collide in the middle

Mrs Blackboot Ha! Caught you at last have we, Ebenezer Blackboot? A fine thing, I must say, running away from your wife and children! Especially when their lives is in danger from a ferocious lion!

Captain Blackboot (*rather sorry that his wife and children have turned up*) I didn't recognise you, Lavinia my dear. Did you recognise them, Mr Mate?

Mate No, I didn't recognise 'em, Cap'n. I thought they was a lot of other people.

Captain Blackboot Mr Bosun?

Bosun Not me, Cap'n. I just 'appened to be looking through the wrong end of my telescope at the time.

Captain Blackboot You see, my love, we didn't recognise you.

Mrs Blackboot Don't you "my love" me, Ebenezer Blackboot! Making your own, dear, innocent children run through the jungle after you! And them with the rampaging measles! It ain't good enough, is it, Cook?

Cook It's a wicked crime, Mum. And if you wants me to bop anyone on the head, I'm ready and willing to bop!

Mrs Blackboot You're a great comfort to me, Cook. Now then children, say "hello" to your Pa!

The children line up as close to Captain Blackboot as possible, and repeat their little verse

Children   Hello Pa,
We've come from far,
In a boat that was tossing and pitching!
Sick as dogs, and cold as frogs,
And oh! how our measles are itching!

Hello Dad,
We feel so bad,
If you kiss us we may not complain!
But you'd better be quick
'Cos we've been very sick,
And it's going to happen again!

Mrs Blackboot Quick! Cook, let's take them behind those trees. Their poor little faces have turned quite green!
Cook Very good, Mum! It's to be hoped as how we're in time.

Cook and Mrs Blackboot hurry the children out of sight

Captain Blackboot sits down on a rock and puts his head in his hands

Captain Blackboot Oh dear, oh dear, oh dear!
Bosun He's upset now.
Captain Blackboot Oh dear, oh dear, oh dearie, dearie, dear
Mate It's the sight of Mrs Captain Blackboot and all them kids wot's done it!
Captain Blackboot Oh dearie, dear. Oh dearie, dearie, dearie, dear.
Bosun Proper upset, 'e is.
Captain Blackboot Oh dearie, dearie, dearie, dearie, dearie, dearie, dear!
Mate Coming on top of everything else, this might well break 'is 'eart.

James, Sally and Victoria come running from the hut

James What a good thing you've come back, Captain. We've got some very important news for you!
Victoria I heard it first!

Sally Be quiet, Victoria. Captain Blackboot, we've found out where Oliver is!

Victoria You mean *I* found it out!

James Don't interrupt, Victoria; He's tied up in one of the caves that belong to the Wreckers!

Victoria And tonight, after they've wrecked a ship, they're going to——

Sally Hush, Victoria! They're going to make him into octopus stew!

Bosun Put him into a pot of boiling salted water? Seasoned with parsley, thyme and grated coconut?

Mate And no-one near enough to 'ear 'is pitiful little screams?

Captain Blackboot Oh dear, oh dear, oh dearie, dearie, dear.

James With respect, Captain Blackboot, it's no good sitting down and saying "oh dear, oh dear, oh dearie, dear." We've got to rescue him. There's no time to be lost!

Victoria That's right. Because as soon as it's dark, these Wreckers are going to——

Sally Let me tell it, Victoria; As soon as darkness falls, these Wreckers are going to sink a ship——

James And creep round to this beach with their beastly lanterns——

Sally And steal all the barrels of brandy from the ship——

James And leave the sailors to drown!

Victoria And *then* make Oliver into octopus stew!!

Sally I've already *told* Captain Blackboot about that!

James And so we *must* think of a plan to frighten away the Wreckers, and rescue Oliver!

Victoria I've got a plan!

Sally Don't be silly.

James How can a little girl like you have a plan that's any good?

Victoria Well, I have! And I was the one who heard what the Wreckers were saying—so I know what would frighten them away!

Mate I think we should listen to the little girl's plan!

Bosun You're right, Mr Mate. So we should!

Mate What do you think, Cap'n?

Captain Blackboot Oh dear, oh dear, oh dearie, dear.

Mate The Captain agrees. Carry on, miss!

Victoria stands up on a rock

Victoria It's like this. The Wreckers can't stand the cry of the Wallamagrumba! The thought of just one Wallamagrumba make them turn pale and tremble and run away as fast as they can! So, if we all learned the cry of the Wallamagrumba, and practised climping and clumping about the beach, they'd run away never to be seen again! And then we could rescue Oliver!

James Not a bad idea, but I don't think there are enough of us to be really frightening.

Mate Don'y you worry about that, Matie. These rows of cheerful souls at high water mark will help us. Won't you, Cheerful Souls?

Audience Yes!

Sally But who's going to teach us the proper cry?

Mate The Bosun's the best one to do that, ain't you Bosun?

Bosun I reckon I am, Mr Mate. My Uncle Charlie used to fair make our blood curdle when 'e imitated the call of the Wallamagrumba.

James Right. Then the Bosun will teach it to us.

Victoria And I'll teach you to climp and clump about the beach, because I'm the only one who's seen a Wallamagrumba!

Sally Don't boast, Victoria.

The Bosun teaches the audience and the people on the stage the awful Wallamagrumba call

Bosun HA!!
Everyone HA!!
Bosun HO!!
Everyone HO!!
Bosun WALLAWALLAWALLAWALLAWALLA!!
Everyone WALLAWALLAWALLAWALLAWALLA!!
Bosun (*in a terrible screeching voice*) YEEEEEEEEEEE!!!
Everyone YEEEEEEEEEEE!!!
Bosun OOOOOOOOWWWWW!!!
Everyone OOOOOOOOWWWWW!!!

They do it until they get it right

Mate Very, very good, maties, all. And now the young lady will
teach us to climp and clump.
Victoria We'd better have some of those heads above high water
mark, to come up here and help us climp and clump.

*The Mate and the Bosun get some children up from the audience,
and following Victoria in a long snake, and yelling the cry of the
Wallamagrumba, they climp and clump about the beach.*

*The Bosun suddenly leaps on to the look-out rock and looks
through his telescope*

Bosun Captain Blackboot, sir! There's a three masted schooner
running in to Skelington Bay! And the Wreckers have lit up
their lanterns!
James Everybody hide!! And when they're all here on the beach
we'll frighten them out of their wits!

Everyone hides. It is getting very dark now

*The Wreckers come creeping on to the beach with their lanterns,
chanting as they come*

Wreckers   We're Wreckers all
               As you can see,
               And we wreck the ships on a stormy sea!
               We run 'em aground
               By lantern light!
               Then we takes our pick
               In the middle of the night!

*The Wreckers raise their lanterns and wave them in the air. James,
followed by everyone, leaps out of hiding, and the loud and
hideous cry of the Wallamagrumba echoes across the beach.
There is great confusion among the Wreckers who are trying to
run away, and quite a bit of hand to hand fighting breaks out.
However, the Wreckers are out-numbered and the Cheerful Souls
are valiant fighters*

Soon, leaving their lanterns behind, the Wreckers flee

Captain Blackboot Well, button up me braces! That was a very
   brave and clever plan that I thought up! Thanks, maties all!
   And now to find Oliver!
James Of course! Now then, Victoria, which cave was Oliver
   in?
Victoria I don't know.
Sally You don't know?
Victoria Of course I don't know! They said he was in a cave, but
   they never said which one!
James I think it was very careless of you to let us go through all
   that shouting and fighting, and still not know where Oliver is!

*Oliver, clutching his red feather duster, comes up from the sea,
followed by the Wallamagrumba*

Oliver Here I am! Here I am!
All (*joyfully*) Oliver! Oliver! Hooray!
Mate Look out matie! There's an ugly looking beast following
   you!
All It's a Wallamagrumba!! Run for your lives!
Oliver Don't be frightened. That's my friend, Wally.
All Wally?
Oliver Yes. He saved my life. He's my best friend. Come up
   here, Wally. No-one will hurt you.

The Wallamagrumba comes up on to the beach

Oliver The Wreckers had a pot of boiling water ready for me.
   They were just sprinkling in the pepper, when Wally heard
   my pitiful cries and swam in through the back of the cave.
   He untied me in the nick of time, then we swam back to his
   house, and Winnie gave us some dinner. Fried winkles. Very
   nice. He'd come to give me my feather duster!
Wally My Winnie didn't want it. She said the feathers would
   make her sneeze!

*Mrs Blackboot enters with Cook and the children. Liza is
wearing the crown*

Mrs Blackboot Now then, Ebenezer Blackboot, what's all this?
Captain Blackboot What's all what, my dear?
Mrs Blackboot There's a large, mangy-looking lion fast asleep on the children's bed, and its chest is covered in measle spots. He looks proper poorly. You should take better care of your friends, Ebenezer Blackboot. I suppose I shall just have to stay here until everyone is better.

Captain Blackboot (*who doesn't mean a word of it*) That will be very nice, my dear.

A row is breaking out among the Blackboot children as to whose turn it is to wear the crown. They are all snatching it from one another when it falls on to the beach. Wally picks it up

Wally This will be the very present for my Winnie. She likes pretty things. I'll just take it home to her. Goodbye, Oliver!

Wally climps and clumps through the audience and exits

The Bosun licks his finger and holds it up

Bosun Cap'n Blackboot, sir, 'tis fifteen bells!
Captain Blackboot Thank you Mr Bosun. Whistle up the crew.
Bosun Ay, ay, sir.
Captain Blackboot Set up the colours, Mr Mate.
Mate (*putting the flag into the ginger beer bottle*) Ay, ay, sir.
Captain Blackboot With the help of the crew and friends, and all you Cheerful Looking Souls at high water mark, we'll sing the dear old song. One, two, three, GO!

The sound of "Rule Britannia" floats across the beach. When the song has finished, the Mate moves down to the audience

Mate Very good you was, maties. Very good! Thank you very much for helping with our play. But it'll be high tide in a few minutes, so if I was you, I'd scarper!!

Black-out

FURNITURE AND PROPERTY LIST

On stage: Rocks. *On them*: three colourful feather dusters
Sand
Long stick. *On it*: notches

Off stage: Union Jack (**Mate**)
Empty ginger-beer bottle (**Mate**)
Telescope. *On it*: red paper stuck to lens (**Bosun**)
Bucket and spade (**Victoria**)
Kegs of rum and brandy (**Wreckers**)
Boxes of treasure (**Wreckers**)
Bottle of medicine and large spoon (**Mrs Blackboot**)
Rolling pin (**Cook**)
Red feather duster (**Wallamagrumba**)
Lanterns (**Wreckers**)

Personal: **Lion**: crown
Captain Blackboot: handkerchief

LIGHTING PLOT

Property fittings required: nil
Exterior. The same scene throughout

To open: Warm, sunny lighting

Cue 1 The three of them make a bolt for it (Page 18)
The sky grows darker and a luminous light appears over the sea

Cue 2 Everyone hides (Page 24)
The sky grows even darker

Cue 3 **Mate:** ". . . I'd scarper!!" (Page 26)
Black-out

EFFECTS PLOT

Cue 1	**Mate:** ". . . to hear us shout like that!" *Wallamagrumba cry*	(Page 4)
Cue 2	**James:** ". . . we'll work out a plan." *Wallamagrumba cry*	(Page 8)
Cue 3	**Bosun:** ". . . frightening us out of our lives!" *Wallamagrumba cry*	(Page 8)
Cue 4	**Captain Blackboot:** "Bring what's left of the feather dusters." *Door being bolted and barred, followed by sinister music*	(Page 8)
Cue 5	**Montague:** "There *is!*" *Wallamagrumba cry*	(Page 13)
Cue 6	**Black Jack:** ". . . I'll show you." *Wallamagrumba cry*	(Page 18)
Cue 7	**Black Jack:** ". . . its ugly teeth." *Wallamagrumba cry even worse than before*	(Page 18)
Cue 8	**Wallamagrumba:** "Winnie!!" *Wallamagrumba cry*	(Page 19)
Cue 9	**Captain Blackboot:** "One, two, three, GO!" *"Rule Britannia"*	(Page 26)